DNA HYMN

annah anti-palindrome

sibling rivalry press
little rock, arkansas
disturb / enrapture

Sibling Rivalry Press, LLC
PO Box 26147
Little Rock, AR 72221

info@siblingrivalrypress.com

www.siblingrivalrypress.com

ISBN: 978-1-943977-21-5

Library of Congress Control No. 2016945234

This title is housed permanently in the Rare Books and Special Collections Vault of the Library of Congress.

First Sibling Rivalry Press Edition, October 2016

For you,
the ones by whom
I've been predisposed

resisting palindromes

/ˈpalin͵drōm/e-
noun

a word, number, sentence, verse, or double stranded sequence of DNA that reads the same backward & forward (anna, see bees, see bees, anna); term is derived from the Greek root "palin dromo," meaning "to run back again," "a recurrence," or "a revolving cycle."

We often reproduce the violent legacies that have been transmitted to us through the unspoken & overarching narratives of our childhoods. While the patterns we learn may define us in some ways, we are also defined by our processes of unpacking, analyzing, & defying those legacies as well.

My mother died in 2007 from a morphine overdose, at which point I changed the spelling of my name from Anna to Annah. This was a cathartic shift for me—a shift which empowered me to break the linguistic pattern that I'd been defined by my entire life—a shift which allowed me to finally resist the life of being a Palindrome.

The concept of Resisting Palindromes has held space for me to challenge the stagnancy I associate with identifying by a given-name I no longer relate to (as I have transformed in drastic ways since it was first assigned to me), & it also reminds me of the commitment I've made to myself, to consciously resist participating in the destructive patterns I've learned over time.

So, if a palindromic name exists as a constrained series of vowels & consonants that preserve an identity via a repetitious, backward/forward pattern, the only way I've found to disrupt this cycle & challenge my assumed predisposition is to add another letter.

anna anna anna anna anna anna anna anna anna anna anna anna anna anna anna anna anna anna anna anna anna anna anna anna anna anna anna anna anna anna anna anna anna anna anna anna anna anna anna anna anna anna anna(h) annah.

To those of you who've so curiously asked over the years why I resist palindromes, please know that it is not a request of those around me, but more a personal vendetta neatly folded up into a mouthful: a daily hymn meant to preserve my integrity—

To keep me Inhabited.

dna hymn

constructing a palindrome

enacting a palindrome

resisting a palindrome

"how does one speak after a violence that literally reconfigures the cellular structure of things, that, in its erasure, records the shadow of what is no longer present?"

—Selah Saterstrom

constructing
a palindrome

DNA hymn is in my hand
salt: a DNA radar and atlas
drowned: a laden word
drown, word
drown my hymn word
DNA hymn is in my hand,
anna

extraction

tooth tile milk moon marrow . clock jaw limb socket hollow .
split hair curl coil crescent . wet nest yolk part swallow .

pupil pond pink rim shore . eyelash bramble black berry sty .
hack saw numb sugar suture . florescent bulb trash ceiling sky .

stiff spine cable skull blossom . mouth house electric fence lips .
carpal tunnel tongue meat shadow . sickle shell slow drain drip .

---

epidural - a local anesthetic administered through spinal tap;
a drug most often used during labor & delivery

b o n e s e t

an infant
has approximately 300 bones

an adult
206

the bones of an infant are pliable
like hot plastic they bend

until graceful dystocia—
an exaltation
of clavicle snaps

        sweet soft skull swamp
        fontanelle

        small bones fuse together
        form heavier ones

sturdy racks
from which to hang
tangled skeins of muscle

trellis cages
to be dressed
in thick vines of tendon

ivory vases
in which organ bulbs soak
before they are returned to the ground

from this we know:
part of us has already chosen
durability over flexibility

from this we know:
we've gifted small parts of ourselves
in the interest of a stronger whole

tenth plague

you robbed him clean that night / left him on the front steps of that unfamiliar stoop / took out half the lawn as you backed into the street with that ugly green van / prayed the thing would make it back to the city in one piece.

you cleared out his bank account / stuffed your pockets full of those bitter yellow pebbles he kept hidden in foil between the mattress & box-spring / threw one pair of clean underwear and some red toeless pumps into a backpack / took off.

you parked the van in that alley between a liquor store & a synagog / stayed pregnant through the last stirs of autumn / slept under the glare of those buzzing florescent street lamps / read your torah portion over & over between shots of whiskey   until the bleeding began

you woke up at first water break / didn't need those doctors or anybody else / reached down & stuck three dirty fingers in / thought of the tenth plague & used your own blood to mark the outside of the van's sliding door: Makat b'chorot

                                                        when a wounded white woman
                                                              is found unconscious
                                                              somebody usually
                                                            takes her to a hospital

you were strapped to that exam table / given a swift kick sting epidural, to which your stiff spine
cable skull blossom sang   amen
it was late november   i was born

                          & you loved me anyways.

---

whiskey

firewood sonata

*Belaruse: a terrible piano—worst piano on
the market; may be disguised under the
names Chubert, Wieler, or Belarusian.*

—*Martha Beth, Piano Brand Review*

my first love rattle wheeze hum
a structure housing echoes
behind wooden breastplate
melodic pneumonia

underneath front shield
steel chords wound tight
obscene mechanics
meant for tuning-surgeons

with sustain pedal croons
you lulled me to sleep
held my cheek against your keys
held my head between C octaves

never said goodbye that december
of frozen copper & warped wood
of sharps & flats misplaced
of rotting mallets & lungs full of mold

dad. axe.
crack. saw.
kindling. coal.
warmth. silence.

you are the reason I can hear songs
in the whistle of a heating vent
in the creak of a door hinge
in the howls
of a wounded animal

gold fever

the california gold rush
began in 1849

within one year's time
the region's most accessible gold
was completely harvested

without gold to sustain their livelihoods
miners became masters at poker card-counting,
pick-pocketing
& general, multipurpose con-artistry

miners who settled into camps
at the base of the sierra foothills—unceded Miwok territory
were said to be particularly restless,
ambitious risk takers who,
despite the lack of gold left in the region,
continued to mine the land
with a frantic & feverish desperation

traffic through the town of placerville
would often be halted by miners
digging holes in the middle of the streets
or wherever they imagined gold to be

they would dig up the floors in their cabins,
pluck gold out of the mortar on buildings
ransack each other's grave sites
praying to catch a dull glint of salvation
amidst the newly turned earth

gold

some say these frenetic mannerisms
have sunk deep into our muscles
clung viscous & wet to our bones

stained the whites of our eyes
a faint golden-red

our parents never stood still
shifted their weight from one leg to the other
ground their teeth down to small ridged stumps
scrounged for change between the couch cushions
like starving, feral cats

our parents were thin
they picked at invisible parasites
crawling along their arms
disappeared every morning
into lots overgrown with dandelions
where all the chemistry shacks stood

our parents taught us to operate metal-detectors
before we even started school
had us scour our front yards
the dusty trenches alongside Highway 50
the gravel banks down by the river
in search of coins, bottle caps,
tangles of stripped copper wire

by the age of ten we could all tell the difference
between pyrite & gold
nickel & cobalt
silver & lead
slugs & quarters

we could smell a scam from a mile away
we knew enough to feel uneasy most of the time
but never to flinch at the sound of jackhammers
on warm summer pavement

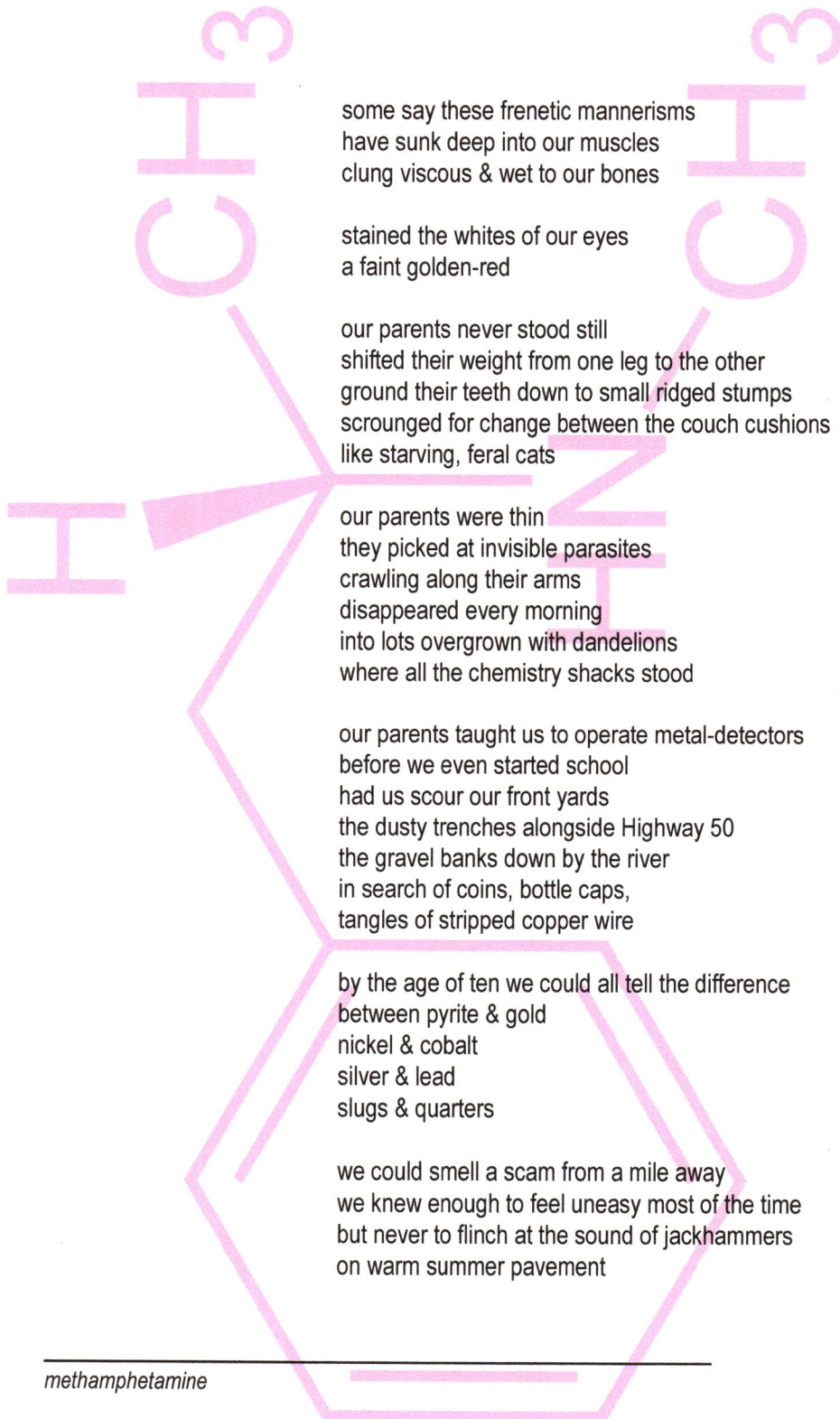

methamphetamine

22

learning to read

to cross a burning bridge:

left right tight rope tip toe stumble . consonant wince vowel split soft stilt stutter . round sound uvula bell noun gag swallow . broken glass breath wet text spit slaughter . tongue boat cathedral throat strangle pray smother . syllable synch verb clench fragment tense solder .

people, much like words, rely on each other for meaning:

left: abandon / left: side . crop: harvest / crop: cut . trip: travel / trip: fall . fall: season / fall: trip . wound: injure / wound: wind . wind: coil / wind: air . object: matter / object: disagree . tear: cry / tear: rip . lead: guide / lead: metal . project: plan / project: throw . key: song / key: lock . bark: tree / bark: dog . hive: rash / hive: honey . construct: build / construct: concept . desert: barren / desert: abandon .

spelling is the clothing of words— their outward, visible expressions—
& they always look good in drag:

i before e except after c . weird is just weird . when ing comes to play e runs away . there is a lie in the word belief . q & u are longterm boos . when two vowels go walking the first one does the talking . a liar lives in the familiar . the silent letter is a bullet proof vest (hidden beneath a cocktail dress) .

ear honey

back flat pressed to clammy bathroom floor, shoulder blades sliced) (into linoleum. *open-your-legs*, she instructed: a non-negotiable command. the porous dark meat of her tongue smacked heavy against her teeth. *open-your-legs*, she slurred again, removed one q-tip from the rectangular cardboard box located on the rusty metal shelf above the sink. i closed my eyes tight: x x: venus flytraps crushing soft bodies of flies. *it's-not-gonna-hurt*, she cooed. her kneecaps popped as she crouched down beside me. *you-know-how-it-feels-good-when-i-clean-out-your-ears?* it was true. when she would circle the soft hollows of my eardrums, massage my equilibrium, i always grew dizzy/rapt/spellbound, enamored by tightly-wound sponges of cotton removed after: warm. sticky. ear-honey, she called it. sometimes there would be blood mixed in with the dull glint of wax—but it was never painful. Lesson #1: blood does not always imply the presence of a wound. Lesson #2: wounds do not always bleed.

progesterone - a steroidal hormone released in the body during the onset of menstruation

middle c

the women who raised us
always squinted like it hurt to look at you

had teeth like weathered piano keys
stained, peeling, umber, brittle
edges usually chipped around Middle C

teeth exhausted from the work of being conduits
for sound to pass through
so relentlessly
for so long

the women who raised us
were obsessed with their CB radios

tuned in religiously several times a day,
seduced interstate truck drivers,
conducted lucrative business transactions

& like oracles
they knew about the most current, local police activity
without ever leaving their front porches

the women who raised us
smoked a lot & punctuated their wet-coughs with laughter

let their tits spill out over elastic tube top fringe
wore budget beauty blood-orange mouth paint
had pores pooled with poorly matched cosmetic paste

had tattooed cursive commemorations
scrawled into the boughs of their necks
& always the sweet stench of a spiral perm

the women who raised us
never made us wipe our koolaid mustaches

tried to teach us how to read using HarlequinRomanceNovels
snuck us sugar cubes under the table during meetings
rolled their eyes during the serenity prayer

those women
always gripped our hands
left half moon shapes in our palms
from cheap acrylic press-on nails))))

& tenderly led us outside to play
anytime a man
said the word Bitch

enacting
a palindrome

sees a most serene rest, serene rest SOMA sees

ann, asleep, peels anna

sleep on no peels

sleep peels

sleep 'til it peels

early escapisms

our moms were always together
guzzling mason jar bloody marys
cackling loudly
cigarettes dangling from the corners
of gaping wet mouths

at first it was ava's idea to play the pass-out game
but then i got hooked too

i always went first
splayed my body across the floor for her
felt the thrill of terror rattle around in my chest as she climbed on top of me
pressed her hands into the sides of my throat

she cut off my air supply & i was in love
sunshine-capillary tint through closed eyelids
raw, pink, viscous
a bowl of salmon roe
a ruptured gestational sac

blood ringing loudly
in a trifecta of minor keys
the waking world drained away
like wet flour through a sieve

became an oceanside of fading bruises
yellow pigment shorelines
cusping a swollen blue tide

when she shook me awake: pop fizz gasp jolt

a soft & tender, plum colored ache
tingly lips & heavy sponge tongue
post asphyxia
intoxication

when ava's mom got sober
they stopped coming around
& when i missed her
i got the shakes

a longing of the nervous system
a longing of the cortex & cerebellum
a longing of the sternum & the pelvis
of the mouth & the tongue

(he)artichoke

after spring slaughter
you vowed
you'd never eat meat again

the thistles that rose from the compost pile
sprouted gaudy prehistoric flower buds
with claws at the tips of its leaves

come dinner table tuesday
greasy mouths agape
we peeled flesh from the bones of our fattest hen
& watched you—instead—eat an artichoke

you plucked leaves from body
like feathers from a warm, dead bird
& sucked at each quill
scraping out small morsels of follicle meat
with your underbite

once all leaves were peeled away
you began devouring a soft
grey
sponge-like stamen

at which point dad told you:

> *the center of an artichoke*
> *is called a heart*

you got up from the table
& just never came back

pavement

we were tough, you & me

we were nails curled in horseshoe shapes
embedded in highway pavement
a monument to soft rubber tires treading above
the limber flexibility of iron,
how defeat smells metallic

nails embedded in highway pavement—no.
we were Pavement.
Pavement, you and me

two girls from the same cavernous confines—
that first small home in the central valley of her torso
the heat was unbearable in there
like sacramento summers
and sizzling jelly-sandals on concrete

those membrane thin walls contracting in
the pulse of guts filtering toxin
a bloodstream nutrient mainlining
rhythmic, retroverted, uterine throbbing

it was a war in there already

we were a battleground of slippery fetal flesh
digestion sounds punctured the fluid of peace
as she passed us amniotic, toxic drinks
ultrasound waves rocked us to sonic, chemical sleep

back when drinking and breathing were the same thing
we were her *Cunning-Baffling-Empowering*

we were flecks of jasmine plastered green to the faces of mom's front teeth
from drinking badly strained tea
at midmorning AA meetings

inside we sat on our tiny hands
with straight faces
listening to mom recount her youth
arrest-after
arrest-after
assault-after-arrest

Rest. Breathe. Rest.
together we were Breath.
we were Breath you and me

& i can remember
Our
first steps

step 1: when she admitted she was *Powerless-Over-Alcohol*,
that her *Life-Had-Become-Unmanageable*

i went to school telling other kids
that our mama was allergic to booze,
she says she breaks out in handcuffs

we were steps 5,6,7 you & me
when we became the other human beings
to whom she admitted the exact nature of her wrongs

& when god wasn't there to remove her *Defects-Of-Character*,
we watched her crawl across a flowerbed
of floral-print linoleum towards us—
hands and knees and belly kissing floor,
trailing scuff-marks from reeking pools of vomit

she: begging amends from her children
like begging repentance from a distracted creator
we were Gods you and me

& we were Junkyard Scavengers
in that huge parking lot
outside the meeting space for hours
collecting shards of broken beer bottle treasures
triangles of beautiful glowing amber
that would shield our eyes
when we looked directly at the sun through them

they were hoarded and traded like coinage
while we truth-or-dared each other into premature age
through the vehicle of boys-we-didn't-even-like
those *Boys-We-Didn't-Even-Like*

but when you became Truth
& i became Dare
we split beyond what sisters-of-pavement pacts could repair
because once you grow up
truth & dare
are opposing ends of a spectrum

i became the runaway
the rehab cliche for which our childhoods sent

i laid the path for what not to do
i became your

Pavement

doorknobs & dead fish

every surface in your trailer
was cluttered with ugly
homemade
ceramic bowls

relics of our childhoods
you felt too guilty to throw away

each bowl was filled to the brim
with brass & steel
palm-sized spheres

appendages dislocated
from the bodies of houses

some had their locks picked out
deep, jagged, hollow wounds
you could see clear through

some had keyholes scabbed over in rust
no longer harboring any intention
to facilitate passage

some had keys stuck in their locks
forever documenting someone's last
arrival or departure

every bowl was filled with doorknobs
except for that lopsided one
on the kitchen table full of water

dry leaves floating on the surface
edges curled in like tiny bassinets

blanketing— wide eyed and still
your dead goldfish

the one gifted to you during your affair
with the town locksmith

p o s t u r e

the sunflower crops
along the Dixon highway
cast sharp
bony silhouettes
against a jaundiced sky

tall slender stalks . tall stiff bodies
somber columns . single file procession
heavy heads hung
from bowing
broken necks

as pockmarked faces gape down
drop loose seeds from their pores
like unanchored teeth
from a fractured jawbone

from this we know:
the posture of grief
can loosen from us
our most vital resources

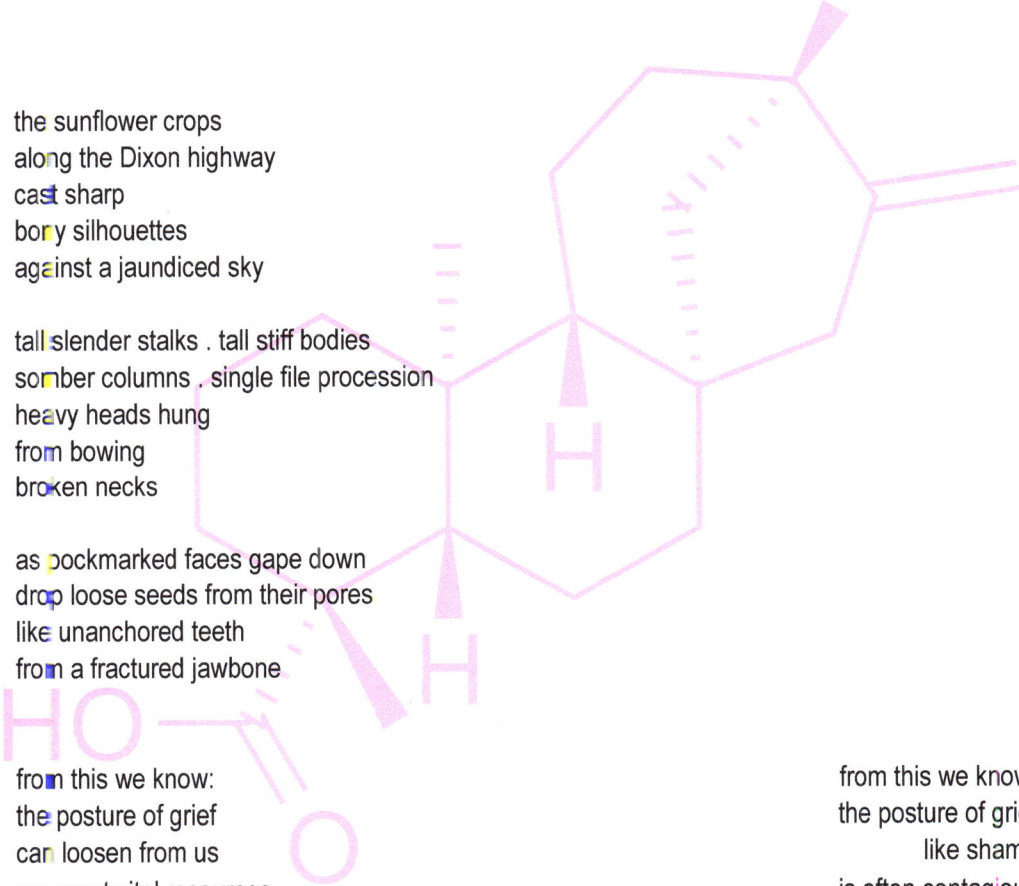

from this we know:
the posture of grief
like shame
is often contagious

---

steviol molecule - a sweetener extracted from the sunflower plant

creosote

the pond was an oval-shaped, aromatic obscenity. a moat overflowing with the neighborhood's bile. green, luminous, rancid.

a fallen pine trunk stretched across the center linking the neighbor's bank to ours like a bridge.

electrical chords tangled in bright yellows, grays, coppers among the blackberry brambles & algae at the pond's shallow edges.

i kept an ever-growing collection of hollow, rusted battery shells found washed up along the shore.

the water was warm & oily. translucent streaks of rainbow swished across the surface amidst fallen leaves & floating cellophane wrappers.

the summer we got hives i was nine & you were five.

a fallen telephone pole had crashed into the pond during the previous winter's storm. leaked new weather-proofing chemicals into the water. our skins glowed the scarlet rashes of a slow, hot sunrise.

hives grew along the column of your spine, resembled ripe, violet-purple grapes swollen along the vine, plump, ready to burst & deflate into the stiff husks of raisins.

we stayed in bed, ate bottles of prednisone & picked at each other until the day the itching finally subsided.

the hives torn open all over my legs were replaced by soft, raised, circular scars.

yours left no trace.

---

creosote - a common wood preservative made from coal-tar

valley to the bay

1989:

the first time i met you
you were breathless & grey
gently swaying
from a navel cord noose   a low swinging pendulum
                                    heavy as copper
                                    slick as motor oil

everyone in the delivery room was freaking out & i thought—
you brilliant little shit

                                    did you just manage to use your own *life line*
                                    as a prop in your first suicide attempt?

oh.

i see you.

1999:

found
washed ashore
with the barren summer pines
& the whimper of a pulse

after you leapt from hangtown bridge
& attempted to swallow
the entire sacramento river

make minnows of your lungs
barnacles of your teeth
white water rapids
of your breath

2010:

found
face down on a piss-stained mattress
cartoon network blasting
from a foil-crowned television set

the hypodermic haunt
of poppy sap
fermenting the blood

                    guts full of soma capsule bobbers
                    in a lake of bile
                    & chocolate milk

gastric lavage
a ritual   a right of passage   a purification

2012:

found

the crushed & overturned shell

of an old jeep wrangler

at the bottom of cedar ravine   with you inside   blood alcohol level

point five oh

2015:

this year
your heart will reach
its 979.1 millionth beat   & my sweet one   despite our best efforts
                                                        some of us
                                                        are just survivors

but oh,
do i see you.

resisting
a palindrome

O dissent i witness, i do

O desire rise, do

are we not drawn onward to new era

are we not drawn onward, we few, drawn onward to new era

annah?

thursday

they say it crept up your throat in the night / you tried to swallow it / take it back / hold it in / keep it down / leave the pillows clean. they say you fed me bowtie noodles with watery ketchup & you went hungry . they say you broke your ankle in the stairwell running behind me with my bags / didn't collapse until i was safely on the train (toward a home you'd never see) . they say you must've been quiet / nobody was stirred from slumber & the sour parable stayed matted in the folds of your lungs until we woke up on our own with the garbage truck.

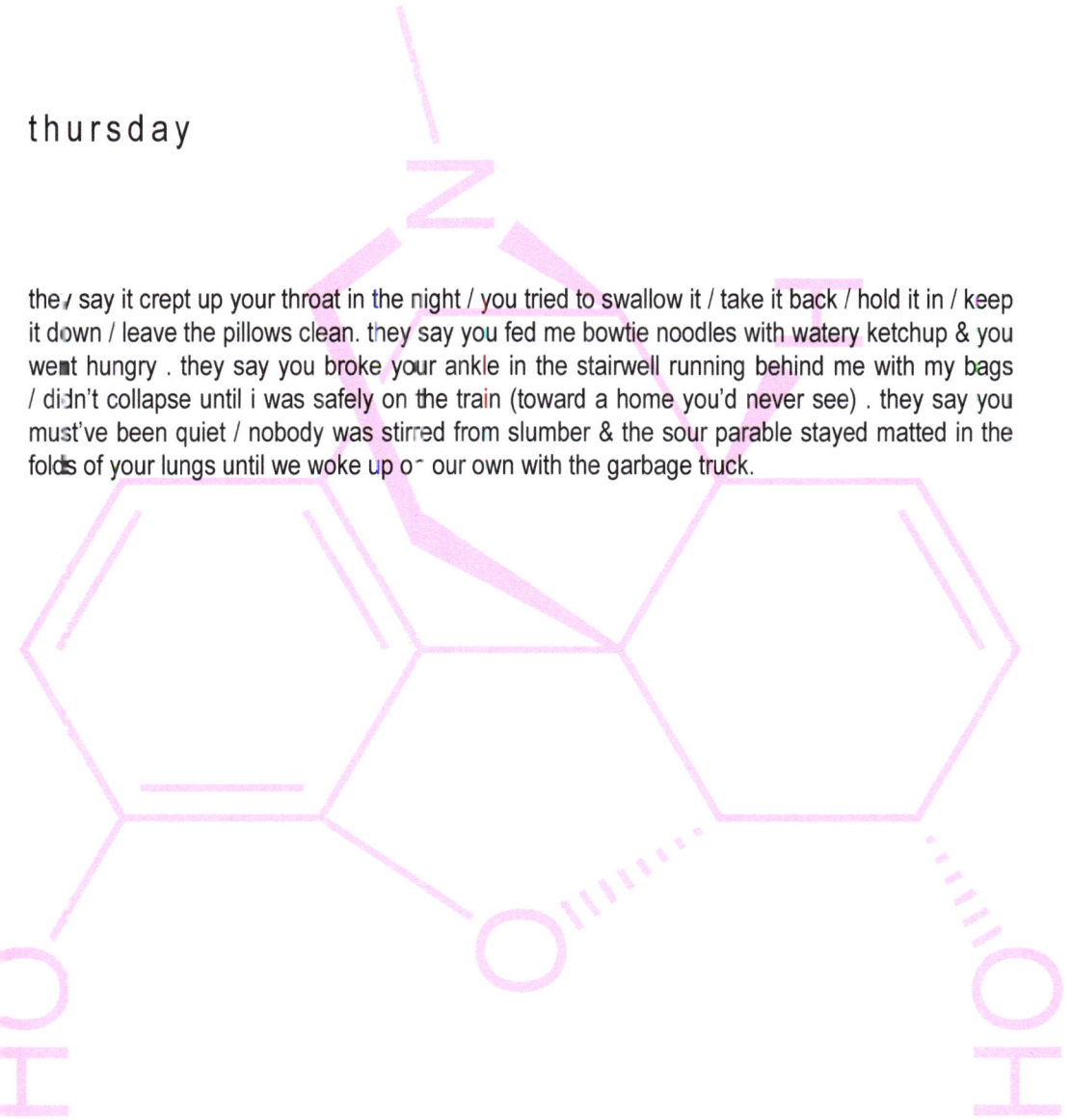

morphine

epigenetic

the blood may contain memories that do not belong to you . blood will never quench the thirst . you cannot get blood from a stone . blood does not boil, curdle or run cold . blood does not have a surname . blood is not young or old or bad or sweet . blood is not royal . the moon does not contain blood . blood baths are not for cleansing . you cannot cry or sweat blood . blood has no affiliation with the nationstate . RH-negative blood can kill the RH-positive fetus . blood has neither citizenship nor political asylum . the roots of orchids thrive on blood meal . bloodshed is one word . having someone's blood on your hands does not always render you guilty . resentment cannot survive in the blood . anemic blood is sometimes thinner than water . blood does not always determine family . blood and lace are perfect together . bloodlines do not always cross . blood is not a map . blood is not an open door . the blood is not a magnet

hymn-noptera vespine

grandpa told us
> bees are the tears of our sun
> that once fell upon desert sand
> and refused to evaporate

grandma told us
> bees are phantom postal workers
> who shuttle messages back and forth
> between the living and the dead

you told us
> when the honey runs dry
> we sacrifice our young—let them rot in the womb
> & from the stillest of births will rise bees to fill our empty hives

---

apamin molecule - bee venom

i found your bed littered with the brittle yellow husks
of a thousand dead hornets

they peppered the quilt you made
with color combinations you never would have chosen

all the windows were sealed shut
there must have been a nest in the wall somewhere

i exhumed each body
made hearses of my palms
dissolved a few in the hot sweat of transit

in the kitchen at home
i enshrined each bee in its own gel-cap casket

one of which i swallow every night before bed

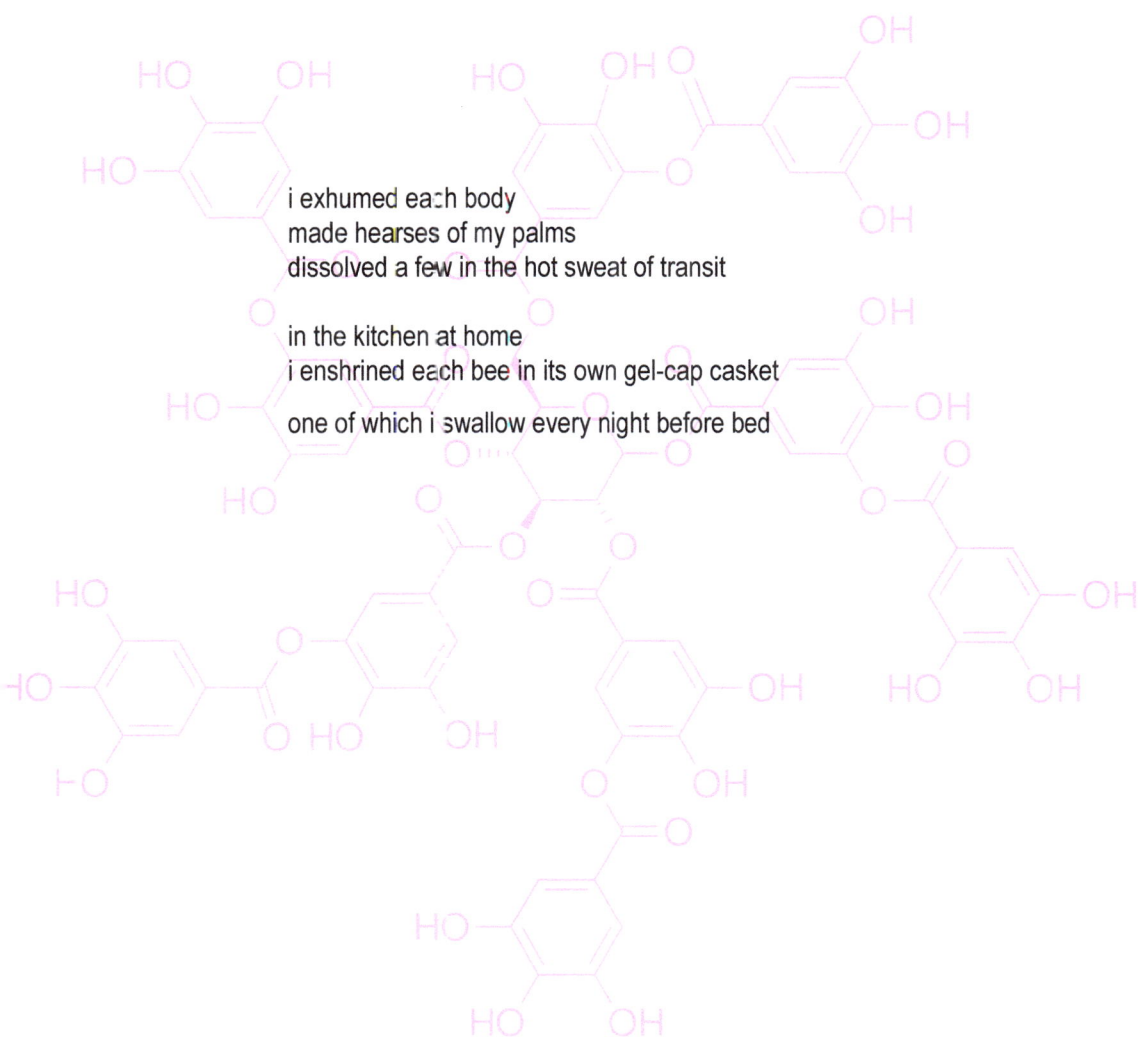

tannic acid - a substance often used topically to pull venom from the skin after a bee sting

s a c c h a r i n

this gender
is someone's unfinished attempt
at cleverly defacing
a misogynistic billboard ad

it's a tampon applicator full of pop rocks
the mace you thought was breath spray
the tattoo you most regret:
a parable of faded   but legible   mistakes

this gender
is your high school english teacher's eyebrows
plucked thin and painted back on
into a perpetual state of concern

it's the spot in your throat that stays dry no matter how many times you swallow
a hymnal measure wrapped around the larynx in sore rasps
the sound of a confession that aches the roots of your teeth
for days after it's told

this gender
is the repurposed scrap fabric
window dressing/ tablecloth/ porch blanket/ nightgown/ miniskirt/ DIY cotton menstrual pad
you now use for the purpose of flagging

it's the sticky-hot flush of finally achieving literacy
the water bottle filled with bleach
sprayed into the eyes of a trucker
who picked you up hitchhiking & refused to let you out when you asked

this gender
is the dated love affair between Tonya Harding & Nancy Kerrigan
a public performance of rivalry & spite used as fodder for a hot scene
back at the hotel, in the judicial court lavatory, & the olympic arena locker room

it's the laxative you finally slipped into your boss's coke
after he harassed you at work for the last time
your mom's secret renegade romance
with her femme dyke hairdresser

this gender

is the unwashed hands of a lover grasping at your most hollow parts
the note between notes that bellows from your throat
when you've finally found the language to tell someone   How   you want to be touched

it's the stray eyelash
the one stuck to your left cheekbone
that you were hoping someone you love
would get close enough to notice

hymn of the pulse

when you sing
your mouth is a hive
open up   open wide
inside your gums
fresh honey resides
pockets to puncture
and drain over time

measure & verse
lurk in your gestures
pitch & tenor
hold fast in your touch
minor scales
animate your limbs
chord progressions
expand your lungs

key of A
key of C
keys to front door locks
cellular echoes
ribcage pulses
and metronome knocks

chest plate hollows
sustained breath &
vibrato tones
a bridge, a chorus
alive between the
skin and the bones

dear, highway 50

i have always loved & hated you

hitching west always filled us with hope. led us toward an orange, sinking belly of sun with throbbing veins & aching gums. your shoulders, slate & shale hunched under heavy shawls of woven wire netting. your shoulders, hosts to a generation of abandoned vehicles devoured by rust & wild poppies. your shoulders were jail-bait stations, we leaned seductively over guardrails and waved our red flags at oncoming traffic. your shoulders were training grounds & crash course terminals, catwalks & boxing rings, harbors & narrative arcs. your shoulders held us while we slept in nests of paper waste & foxtail thistle, nests of broken bones and weeping hides. hitching east always filled us with poise. brought us home toward a hot white sunrise with tissue paper eyelids, glass cleaner breath, rubber band tongues & stiff, aching necks.

mullein

mullein is a plant that only grows in disturbed areas

along riverbeds
where rapids gnaw at bank

under highway guardrails
where pavement scabs against soil

on steep hillsides
where loose dirt threatens avalanche

the roots of mullein repair ground
hold landscapes together for other things to grow

from this we know:
in the presence of trauma
remarkable survival mechanisms
flourish

from this we know:
at the edges of impact
there is always a sweet spot
between calloused & bleeding

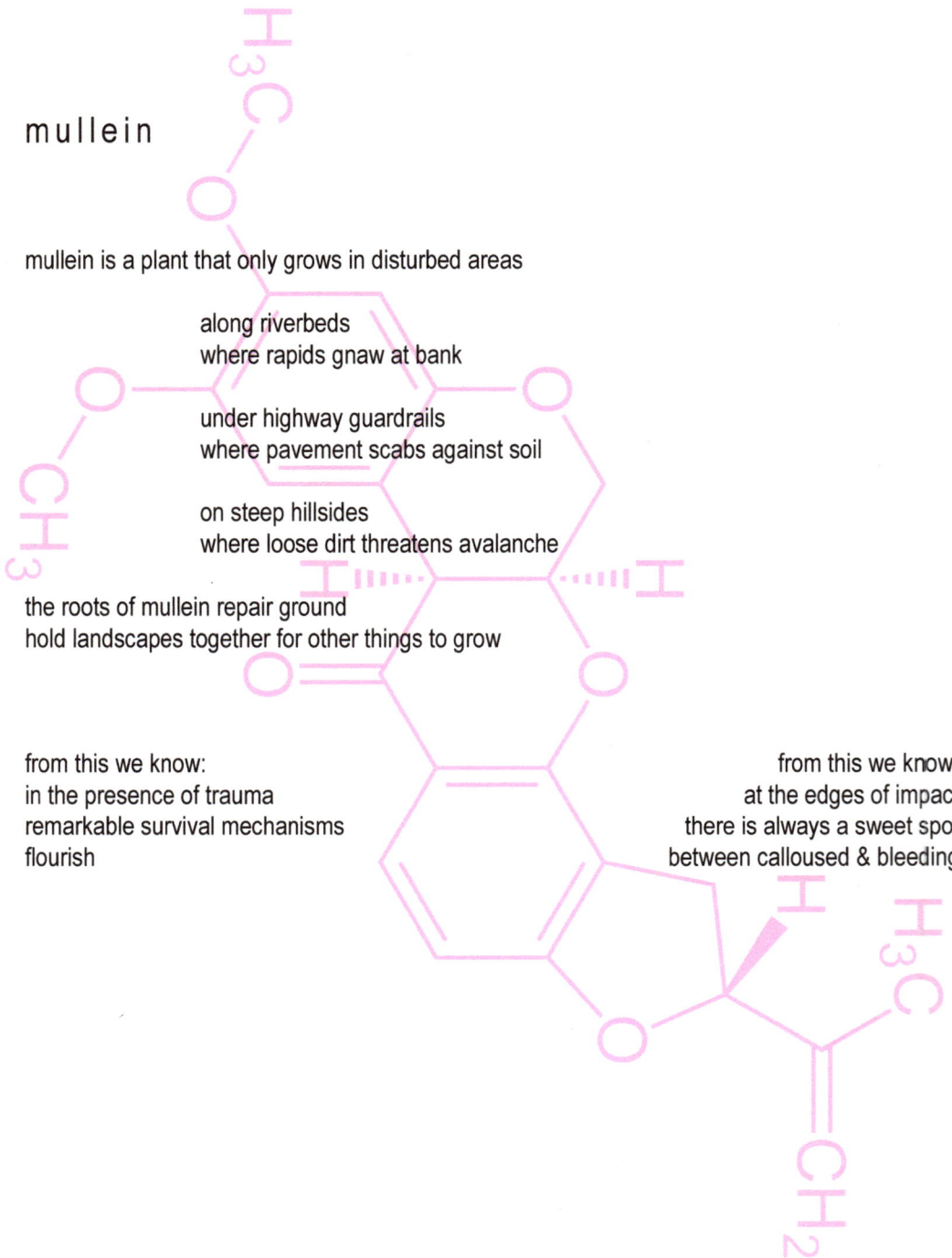

rotenone - a chemical found in the seeds of mullein; a substance often used as a paralytic fish poison

DNA HYMN

notes

gold fever

> page one of this poem contains found text from *Dry Diggins* by K.L. Hemley

learning to read

> page one of this poem is in conversation with Kofi Annan's quote, "literacy is a bridge from misery to hope." / page three is in conversation with Mary Norris' quote, "spelling is the clothing of words."

epigenetic

> epigenetic: the presence of ancestral memory in the blood
> poem written with undying gratitude, love, & devotion for Randall Scott Wilson
> poem in conversation with Sossity Chiricuzio's quote, "the blood is not a magnet"

extraction

> former version of this poem was published in *Emerge: 2015 Lambda Fellows Anthology*

tenth plague

> Makat b' chorot: number ten of the ten plagues, "plague of the first born"

hymn-noptera vespine

> title based on the term hymenoptera vespinae—a subfamily of insect that includes all eusocial wasps including bees, hornets, yellow-jackets, etc.
> former version of this poem was published in *Emerge: 2015 Lambda Fellows Anthology*

saccharin

> written in loving memory of Leslie Feinberg
> & with reverence & solidarity for Minnie Bruce Pratt
> former version of this poem published in *Glitter & Grit: Queer Performance from the Heels on Wheels Femme Galaxy*

hymn of the pulse

> for Jerre B. Fine, the other one who—in the face of trauma—taught himself how to sing

dear, highway 50

> former version of this poem published in *Passage & Place: Queer Writings on Home*

pavement

> former version of this poem published in *Transfer Magazine*

acknowledgments

DNA Hymn was written on unceded, occupied Ohlone, Miwok, Shahaptian, & Tongva land.

I'd like to thank Bryan Borland for being such an inspiring, bad-ass poet & co-conspirator, & Sibling Rivalry Press for giving me the opportunity to publish my first book.

Thanks to those of you who, through the precision of your close reads, edits, and feedback, have helped me perform countless surgeries and resurrections on this project over the years.

Thanks to every survivor & freedom fighter & country-trash, revolutionary femme who taught me how (and when) to use a switchblade. Thanks to all the poor & working-class women in Placerville whose invisible labor provided us with food, shelter, transportation, & safety when we were kids. Thanks to every queer archivist, activist, artist, & antagonist whose refusal to disappear has taught us to take our own voices to the page in revolt.

Thanks to my queer family, who has held me so tight, held me accountable, held me together, & held me with so much fucking love that I've felt unbreakable even in the midst of some pretty garish times. Thanks to my teachers & mentors who've pushed me to my fullest capacities, kept me honest, and inspired me beyond words with their own brilliant work. Thanks to Randy Wilson, without whom, I'm sure I wouldn't exist. Thanks to the 12 step communities who took such good care of my mom every time she was washed up on the shores of her addiction. Thanks to my siblings for staying the fuck alive. And thanks to my mother, Elisabeth Anne Yomtob Wilson, for everything—but especially for the gift of literacy—a gift that has continued to keep my heart well & beating all this time.

Many of you overlap with these categories, but for the sake of diligence, thank you to: The Washington Wilsons, Alina Drummond, Sara & Randall, Sunny Drake, Jezebel Delilah X, Leahjo & Berkley Carnine, Alex Holding, Imogen Binnie, Aviv Gerber, Encian Pastel, Rebekah Edwards, Voula O'clock, Lex Non-Scripta, Malic Amalya, Susanne Boehm, Truong Tran, Lambda Literary's 2015 poetry cohort, C. Russell Price, Kazim Ali, Meg Day, Seeley Quest, Ash Ebbo, Ayah Young, Pocket Mycat, Charles Arpe, Ariel Springfield, Leah Lakshmi Piepzna Samarasinha, Naamen

Tilahun, Jerre B. Fine, Ri Molnar, The Peeblers, Juliana Spahr, Deborah Cohler, Jillian Sandell, Kernan Willis, Ledah Wilcox, Koralie Hill, J Walk, Lewis Wallace, Etta Cetera, Simon Strikeback, Franciszka Fierce, The Lady Miss Vagina Jenkins, Anne & Bill Ekes, Molly McIntyre, Kelly Short&Queer, Mia McKenzie, Gina @ Liminal, & *Everyday Feminism*…

Due to space restrictions I'm unable to list the names of everybody I'm grateful for here, but hopefully you know who you are. From the bottom of my little thumper: Thank you.

Love & Rage,

Annah

about the poet

Annah Anti-Palindrome is a working-class/hard-femme/JewWitch sound-artist & writer from California currently living in the San Francisco Bay Area. These days she spends most of her time snuggling with her cat, doing clinical reproductive justice advocacy, and fighting the white-supremacist-capitalist-heteropatriarchy through art activism!

Annah holds an MFA degree from Mills College. She is a Lambda Literary Fellow, a staff writer for *Everyday Feminism*, and a member of Oakland's Deviant Type Press Collective. She has toured with her work throughout the US and Canada, her writing has appeared in a number of anthologies, and she's released three full length albums of music—*White Knuckle Sonnets*, *An(n)a(h)log*, and *Dangling Modifiers*. For more info about Annah, see www.annahantipalindrome.com.

about the press

Sibling Rivalry Press is an independent press based in Little Rock, Arkansas. It is a sponsored project of Fractured Atlas, a nonprofit arts service organization. Contributions to support the operations of Sibling Rivalry Press are tax-deductible to the extent permitted by law, and your donations will directly assist in the publication of work that disturbs and enraptures. To contribute to the publication of more books like this one, please visit our website and click *donate*.

www.ingramcontent.com/pod-product-compliance
Lightning Source LLC
Chambersburg PA
CBHW060859090426
42737CB00024B/3492